PRAYERS & PROMISES

for

WISDOM

BroadStreet
PUBLISHING

CONTENTS

INTRODUCTION

When life asks unending questions and you begin to
feel overwhelmed by the many decisions you have to
make, bring all of your concerns to God. You can take
comfort knowing that he is the author and creator of
all that exists, and he cares deeply for you. He always
knows what is best.

Prayers & Promises for Wisdom incorporates seventy
different themes to help you receive the inspiration
found in the promises of God's Word. Uplifting prayers
and questions offer an opportunity for deeper reflection.

Begin to experience underlying joy and peace as you
let the wise and wonderful promises of God guide you.

ACCEPTANCE

"The Father gives me the people who are mine.
Every one of them will come to me,
and I will always accept them."

JOHN 6:37 NCV

The LORD does not see as man sees;
for man looks at the outward appearance,
but the LORD looks at the heart.

1 SAMUEL 16:7 NKJV

If God is for us, who can be against us?

ROMANS 8:31 ESV

Before he made the world, God chose us to be his very
own through what Christ would do for us; he decided
then to make us holy in his eyes, without a single fault—
we who stand before him covered with his love.

EPHESIANS 1:4 TLB

*Lord, your kindness toward me abounds as I sit here and
know that I am forever accepted by you—nothing can change
that. You know the list of fear, the lack of faith, stacked
against me, yet you still choose to call me your own. As this
truth sinks in my heart, help me to accept with the same love
my family in Christ. Though I disagree with people, help
me to lay down my rights, as you did yours, to serve in love.
I need more of your love-fueled wisdom to show me how to
navigate these relationships well.*

When you apply God's wisdom in situations, how are you more accepting of others?

ANGER

Don't get angry.
Don't be upset; it only leads to trouble.
Evil people will be sent away,
but those who trust the LORD will inherit the land.

PSALM 37:8-9 NCV

Everyone should be quick to listen, slow to speak
and slow to become angry, because human anger
does not produce the righteousness that God desires.

JAMES 1:19-20 NIV

"Don't sin by letting anger control you."
Don't let the sun go down while you are still angry.

EPHESIANS 4:26 NLT

I want to grow in wisdom, Lord. Your Word tells me that one who is quick-tempered is foolish—the opposite of wisdom! I don't want to be a person controlled by anger. Search me, oh God, and find within me the root of this outrage. Help me consider my ways, to pause before I speak, and to slow down enough to understand what is going on in my heart. Dig out of my heart any roots of bitterness. May the only thing that controls me be your Spirit. Let my responses to those around me produce righteousness.

How does the wisdom of God help you from responding in anger?

ANXIETY

You will keep in perfect peace
those whose minds are steadfast,
because they trust in you.

ISAIAH 26:3 NIV

"Don't let your hearts be troubled.
Trust in God, and trust also in me."

JOHN 14:1 NLT

Give all your worries to him,
because he cares about you.

1 PETER 5:7 NCV

I call out to the LORD when I'm in trouble,
and he answers me.

PSALM 120:1 NIRV

I sit before you, compassionate Father, with hands open, palms up. This is the posture of release, and I release my anxiety to you. Calm my body; still my soul. This burden I hand to you. I also come, in full expectation for you to give me the wisdom for this situation that is causing me unease. Walk with me step by step, hand in hand. Bring freedom from the fear that threatens to ensnare me on this journey. I want to tell you what I'm thankful for right now as I war against the anxiety. I remember how much I have to be grateful for and how faithful you have been to me in the past.

What steps can you take to be less anxious and more trusting?

ASSURANCE

To him who is able to do immeasurably more than all we
ask or imagine, according to his power that is at work
within us, to him be glory... for ever and ever! Amen.

EPHESIANS 3:20–21 NIV

All of God's promises have been fulfilled in Christ
with a resounding "Yes!"

2 CORINTHIANS 1:20 NLT

Jesus Christ is the same yesterday and today and forever.

HEBREWS 13:8 NASB

These things I have written to you who believe in the
name of the Son of God, that you may know that you have
eternal life, and that you may continue to believe in the
name of the Son of God.

1 JOHN 5:13 NKJV

Father, doubt is a storm that seems as though it can capsize me. When guided by my own feelings and thoughts, I may surely drown. You are firm ground; your words are a lighthouse. Your power can stop the waves and bring my soul to stillness. Let these verses and your whole Word be stepping stones to dry land. Keep them near my heart and let them pour from my lips. I choose truth to lead the way in dark times. Let faith arise, grow, and bear fruit—a confident assurance of your work in me. Thank you for your Spirit within me, sealing me until the end.

How does believing God's promises cause you to feel reassured?

BELIEF

"For God so loved the world that he gave his one and only Son, that whoever believes in him shall not perish but have eternal life. For God did not send his Son into the world to condemn the world, but to save the world through him. Whoever believes in him is not condemned."

JOHN 3:16, 18 NIV

To all who did accept him and believe in him he gave the right to become children of God.

JOHN 1:12 NCV

Believe on the Lord Jesus Christ, and you will be saved, you and your household.

ACTS 16:31 NKJV

"All things are possible to him who believes."

MARK 9:23 NASB

God of miracles, of all-power and wisdom and might, I remind myself today of who you are. I ponder the powerful works you have done through the ages, and in my own life. Let this stir up belief inside of me. Help my unbelief! Your Word says that belief comes by hearing the Word of God. Help me apply this truth by giving me an appetite for your Word— an insatiable hunger. Soften my heart to be able to receive your truth. Let not the seeds of wisdom fall on soil that isn't ready to receive.

How does God's wisdom help strengthen your belief in God?

BOLDNESS

He proclaimed the kingdom of God
and taught about the Lord Jesus Christ—
with all boldness and without hindrance!

ACTS 28:31 NIV

Sinners run away even when no one is chasing them.
But those who do what is right are as bold as lions.

PROVERBS 28:1 NIRV

On the day I called you, you answered me.
You made me strong and brave.

PSALM 138:3 NCV

Let us come boldly to the throne of our gracious God.
There we will receive his mercy,
and we will find grace to help us
when we need it most.

HEBREWS 4:16 NLT

You are the God of all access. Through your work on the cross, Jesus, I can now approach the throne with complete confidence that you want me there, you hear me, and you care deeply about my needs. Help me to view you as full of mercy and grace, since my tendency is to shy away in fear. Free me from the bondage of fear that separates me from you. This portrait of you on the throne full of mercy and grace reassures me that you have my best interest in mind. Help me pray unaltered and unashamed, wait with patience, and then act in the wisdom of your Word.

Why do you need wisdom to be bold?

CHANGE

Look! I tell you this secret:
We will not all sleep in death,
but we will all be changed.

1 CORINTHIANS 15:51 NCV

He will take our weak mortal bodies and change them
into glorious bodies like his own, using the same power
with which he will bring everything under his control.

PHILIPPIANS 3:21 NLT

Jesus Christ is the same yesterday and today and forever.

HEBREWS 13:8 NIRV

God of majestic mountain tops and serene valleys, nothing is outside your scope of vision. Here on earth our mortality makes change hard, the unknown fearful. But you are immortal, all knowing, the sovereign God who weaves together our lives into a beautiful tapestry for your glory. Change is inevitable if we are to grow. As you continue to sanctify me through the highpoint and valleys of life, thank you for the reality that you will one day finish the process; the change will be complete and I will be complete in you. Until that day, let me rest in the assurance that you are in control of all things.

How do you handle change better with God's wisdom?

CHILDREN

Direct your children onto the right path,
and when they are older, they will not leave it.

Proverbs 22:6 nlt

"These words which I command you today shall be
in your heart. You shall teach them diligently to your
children, and shall talk of them when you sit in your
house, when you walk by the way, when you lie down,
and when you rise up."

Deuteronomy 6:6–7 nkjv

"Let the little children come to Me,
and do not forbid them;
for of such is the kingdom of heaven."

Matthew 19:14 nkjv

Children are a gift from the Lord;
they are a reward from him.

Psalm 127:3 nlt

Holy Spirit, it is only by your power that I can produce fruit—love, joy, peace, patience, goodness, faithfulness, gentleness, and self-control. This is how I know I should respond to your children; yet without you I fail to do so every time. Will you fill me with your love for those in my care who are difficult? Reassure me in peace, when things feel out of control, and ground me in patience in my moment-by-moment tasks. Help me fix my eyes on your goodness. Enable me to persevere faithfully in the most mundane tasks. Equip me to be gentle in my correction and self-controlled in my responses.

How can you respond to the children in your care with wisdom?

COMFORT

God's dwelling place is now among the people,
and he will dwell with them.
"He will wipe every tear from their eyes.
There will be no more death"
or mourning or crying or pain,
for the old order of things has passed away.

REVELATION 21:3–4 NIV

May our Lord Jesus Christ himself and God our Father,
who loved us and by his grace gave us eternal comfort
and a wonderful hope, comfort you and strengthen you.

2 THESSALONIANS 2:16–17 NLT

To all who mourn he will give: beauty for ashes;
joy instead of mourning; praise instead of heaviness.
For God has planted them like strong and
graceful oaks for his own glory.

ISAIAH 61:3 TLB

Jesus, these verses remind me of the comfort of home. The warmth, the personal nature, the way when I'm home I can be myself completely, all masks off. What is far more beautiful than this is that you have come to earth as a baby, lived a sinless life, died for my sin, and resurrected with the power over death all so you could dwell with me—so that we could abide together. I invited you in, Jesus; come make your home with me. Move right in and make yourself at home. Illuminate my heart as a dwelling place with you.

How does God's wisdom bring you comfort?

CONFIDENCE

I can do everything through Christ,
who gives me strength.

PHILIPPIANS 4:13 NLT

Be my rock of refuge, to which I can always go;
give the command to save me,
for you are my rock and my fortress.
For you have been my hope, Sovereign LORD,
my confidence since my youth.

PSALM 71:3, 5 NIV

Do not throw away your confidence,
which has a great reward.

HEBREWS 10:35 NCV

God you are faithful and true. The book of James tells me that those who doubt are tossed about like waves in the sea. Your Word describes you, however, as a fortress. What a contrast! When I am in you, then I am strong. You are not influenced by the outside disturbances like I so often can be. You are timeless and solid. I know I can put my trust fully in you, that you are good on your promises. Thank you for these wonderful truths! I praise you for keeping my feet on solid ground.

How does having God's wisdom increase your confidence?

CONTENTMENT

To enjoy your work and to accept your lot in life—
that is indeed a gift from God. The person who does that
will not need to look back with sorrow on his past,
for God gives him joy.

ECCLESIASTES 5:20 TLB

I know what it is to be in need,
and I know what it is to have plenty.
I have learned the secret of being content
in any and every situation,
whether well fed or hungry,
whether living in plenty or in want.
I can do all this through him who gives me strength.

PHILIPPIANS 4:12-13 NIV

Empty handed I entered this world, and empty handed I will come home to you, Father. Everything I have, every breath I take, I recognize as a gift given to me from you. You have blessed me richly! In you there is adventure beyond my wildest dreams—relationship with you is enough to sustain me for a lifetime. When I feel restless, open my eyes to the boundless depths that you and I can go. When I falter to be discontent about my mere earthly possessions, remind me again that none of it is my own. Thank you for relationship with you and for every gift you give.

How does wisdom help you choose to be content with your life?

COURAGE

Be strong in the Lord and in his mighty power.
Put on the full armor of God, so that you can
take your stand against the devil's schemes.

EPHESIANS 6:10-11 NIV

Be alert. Continue strong in the faith.
Have courage, and be strong. Do everything in love.

1 CORINTHIANS 16:13-14 NCV

Even though I walk through the darkest valley,
I will not be afraid. You are with me.
Your shepherd's rod and staff comfort me.

PSALM 23:4 NIRV

"This is my command—be strong and courageous!
Do not be afraid or discouraged.
For the LORD your God is with you wherever you go."

JOSHUA 1:9 NLT

Father, you are not a hands-off God; you are working mightily in our world today. Grant me the courage to see where you are moving and to partner with you. Here I am, Lord, send me! I know that you have made me the person for this job. You have called me here, so I pray for courage to take action. Thank you that you desire to partner with me; thank you that I get to be a vessel for your glory. Let nothing hinder me from walking out in boldness for the tasks you have for me today.

How does God's wisdom give you more courage?

COURTESY

Each of us should please our neighbors for their good,
to build them up. For even Christ did not please himself
but, as it is written: "The insults of those who insult you
have fallen on me."

<small>ROMANS 15:2-3 NIV</small>

Welcome strangers, because some who have done this
have welcomed angels without knowing it.

<small>HEBREWS 13:2 NCV</small>

Remind God's people to obey rulers and authorities.
Remind them to be ready to do what is good.
Tell them not to speak evil things against anyone.
Remind them to live in peace.
They must consider the needs of others.
They must always be gentle toward everyone.

<small>TITUS 3:1-2 NIRV</small>

You, Jesus, being in the very form of God, humbled yourself so completely as to come to earth as a baby. You displayed true humility for me. Please forgive me for the times when I am self-centered and unkind to others. When my opinions are more important than love, silence my tongue. When I cower inward to protect myself, instead of reaching out to a stranger in need, push me out of my comfort zone. Help me to see other people as the people you created in your image and died for. Help me to respect you in them and learn to love selflessly.

How does God's wisdom help in your attempt to be courteous to others?

CREATIVITY

Lᴏʀᴅ, you have made many things;
with your wisdom you made them all.
The earth is full of your riches.

PSALM 104:24 NCV

We are God's masterpiece.
He has created us anew in Christ Jesus,
so we can do the good things
he planned for us long ago.

EPHESIANS 2:10 NLT

The Lᴏʀᴅ has filled him with the Spirit of God.
He has filled him with wisdom,
with understanding, with knowledge
and with all kinds of skill.

EXODUS 35:31 NIRV

We have different gifts,
according to the grace given to each of us.

ROMANS 12:6 NIV

Father, you are a creative God—speaking the world into existence, forming man from dust. You are a potter with hands on my clay heart, a musician with rhythms that this world walks by. I praise you that your imaginative wonder runs so deep, I can see your creation time and time again and be left in constant awe. Inspire me with vision. Give me the courage to pursue what you open my eyes to and boldness to open the gifts you have already given to me. I want to partner with you on a journey into inventive worship.

How can you use your creativity for God?

DELIVERANCE

I waited patiently for the LORD;

he turned to me and heard my cry.

He lifted me out of the slimy pit,

out of the mud and mire;

he set my feet on a rock

and gave me a firm place to stand.

He put a new song in my mouth,

a hymn of praise to our God.

Many will see and fear the LORD;

and put their trust in him.

PSALM 40:1–3 NIV

Humble yourselves in the sight of the Lord,

and He will lift you up.

JAMES 4:10 NKJV

The righteous person faces many troubles,

but the LORD comes to the rescue each time.

PSALM 34:19 NLT

Jesus, you are my deliverer. Thank you for delivering me from the bondage of sin and death and setting the captives free! Sometimes fear and darkness still closes in around me. I plead your blood over these times. Deliver me from the darkness that oppresses me and bring me into a spacious place. You are the good shepherd—always looking out for me and protecting me. I know I can rely on you. There is nothing that can separate me from your love. You will go to the greatest lengths to protect one of your sheep.

How do you seek deliverance from your fears?

DEPRESSION

The Lord hears his people when they call to him for help.
He rescues them from all their troubles.

PSALM 34:17 NLT

Why am I so sad? Why am I so upset?
I should put my hope in God
and keep praising him.

PSALM 42:11 NCV

You, O Lord, are a shield about me,
my glory, and the lifter of my head.

PSALM 3:3 ESV

He has delivered us from the power of darkness
and conveyed us into the kingdom of the Son of His love.

COLOSSIANS 1:13 NKJV

I cry out to you, God, in my sadness, though it takes all my strength, I speak your name: Jesus! Be near. Do you have balm to comfort my soul? Do you know the depths of this hole? I feel alone, but now I will speak what is true: I am never alone—you are so very near. You will not abandon me. The darkness is not dark to you (let your radiance brighten this place). I don't have strength to fight this battle alone. Will you bring others alongside me to help me lift my eyes to you? You will never let go of me.

How do you sense God's comfort in the middle of your sadness?

ETERNITY

We are citizens of heaven,
where the Lord Jesus Christ lives.
And we are eagerly waiting for him
to return as our Savior.

PHILIPPIANS 3:20 NLT

"If I go and prepare a place for you,
I will come back and take you to be with me
that you also may be where I am."

JOHN 14:3 NIV

That will happen in a flash,
as quickly as you can wink an eye.
It will happen at the blast of the last trumpet.
Then the dead
will be raised to live forever.
And we will be changed.

1 CORINTHIANS 15:52 NIRV

Before the world began, you were, God. When this world is gone, you will still be. You are the Alpha and the Omega, beginning and the end. It's hard to comprehend: you blow my mind! Give me strength to live for the age to come, not for the temporary, fleeting pursuits of the here and now. Fill me with expectant joy at the thought of what is coming—a contagious hope that enables me to persevere and run my race well. If need be, realign my priorities. Thank you that I get to spend eternity with you!

Can you view eternity with a hopeful, happy heart, fully trusting in the wisdom of God?

EXCELLENCE

Finally, my brothers and sisters,
always think about what is true.
Think about what is noble, right and pure.
Think about what is lovely and worthy of respect.
If anything is excellent or worthy of praise,
think about those kinds of things.

PHILIPPIANS 4:8 NIRV

By his divine power, God has given us everything we
need for living a godly life. We have received all of this by
coming to know him, the one who called us to himself by
means of his marvelous glory and excellence.

2 PETER 1:3 NLT

The answer is, if you eat or drink,
or if you do anything,
do it all for the glory of God.

1 CORINTHIANS 10:31 NCV

I am secure in you, Jesus. My identity is found in you and my salvation is in you; there is no need for me to strive to achieve anymore. Thank you for the sweet relief of this truth, for the peace it brings. You have given me gifts and placed me around the people I am supposed to influence for your glory. In all tasks, large or small, mundane or adventuresome, I pray that I will give my all. I pray you will guide me as I work daily, letting each task be for your kingdom, for your glory, and not for my own.

How does wisdom help you to be excellent at what you do?

FAITH

Through Christ you have come to trust in God. And you have placed your faith and hope in God because he raised Christ from the dead and gave him great glory.

1 PETER 1:21 NLT

"Because your faith is much too small. What I'm about to tell you is true. If you have faith as small as a mustard seed, it is enough. You can say to this mountain, 'Move from here to there.' And it will move. Nothing will be impossible for you."

MATTHEW 17:20 NIRV

The important thing is faith—
the kind of faith that works through love.

GALATIANS 5:6 NCV

Faith is confidence in what we hope for
and assurance about what we do not see.

HEBREWS 11:1 NIV

El Shaddai, you are all sufficient, and I praise you. You are the one true God: the living God, holy and seated on the throne. There is nothing outside of your power. You are the way-maker, and all creation is in submission to you. These powerful truths cause faith to rise in me. Nothing is impossible with you! Where I lack faith, fill me up again. I confess at times I feel I have no faith. Give me the wisdom to work it out, to wrestle through it. I know you are holding onto me and will never let go.

How does wisdom help your faith in Jesus?

FAITHFULNESS

Your lovingkindness, O LORD, extends to the heavens,
Your faithfulness reaches to the skies.

PSALM 36:5 NASB

The Lord is faithful,
who will establish you
and guard you from the evil one.

2 THESSALONIANS 3:3 NKJV

LORD, you are my God;
I will exalt you and praise your name,
for in perfect faithfulness
you have done wonderful things,
things planned long ago.

ISAIAH 25:1 NIV

The word of the LORD is upright,
and all his work is done in faithfulness.

PSALM 33:4 ESV

I am overflowing with gratitude for your consistency in my life, Lord. You do not shift amidst my popcorn thoughts. You are not swayed by popular opinion or faltered by my capricious feelings. I look backwards and mark with grateful praise the evidence of your faithfulness in my life. I look forward in confidence that you will remain faithful. And I request that in the present time you fill me with hope at the wonderful works you are doing in my life. I choose to trust you, to submit my will to your will, because I know you are loyal to your promises.

How have you seen the faithfulness of God played out in your life?

FEAR

The LORD is my light and my salvation—
whom shall I fear?
The LORD is the stronghold of my life—
of whom shall I be afraid?

PSALM 27:1 NIV

We can say with confidence,
"The LORD is my helper,
so I will have no fear.
What can mere people do to me?"

HEBREWS 13:6 NLT

When I am afraid, I will trust you.
I praise God for his word.
I trust God, so I am not afraid.
What can human beings do to me?

PSALM 56:3-4 NCV

Father, wisdom is your gentle voice telling me you are near so I need not be afraid. Countless times in Scripture you tell me not to be afraid. I remember these truths: fear pushes me, but you desire to lead me. Fear overwhelms me and feels heavy; your burden is light and you comfort me. Help me to notice the outworking of fear: the emotions and feelings that might be rooted in fear. Give me discernment to work through them, to overcome them, and to shout into the darkness, "Whom shall I fear? I trust God!"

What fears can you fight with God's wisdom right now?

FORGIVENESS

"If you forgive other people when they sin against you,
your heavenly Father will also forgive you."

MATTHEW 6:14 NIV

Put up with each other.
Forgive one another if you are holding
something against someone.
Forgive, just as the Lord forgave you.

COLOSSIANS 3:13 NIRV

He is so rich in kindness and grace
that he purchased our freedom
with the blood of his Son
and forgave our sins.

EPHESIANS 1:7 NLT

God, wisdom says that not forgiving someone doesn't hurt them; it only damages me. Your Word tells me that bitterness rots my soul. Let this knowledge translate into my heart language. Help me to forgive. I trust in your experience as the one who has forgiven all. Help me follow in your footsteps however big they may feel. Guard my heart against the bitter root and shield me from a hardened heart. I am in wonder at your deep mercy; there is none like you that would choose to die for a sinner like me or like those who hurt me. Thank you for your sacrifice, your example, and your forgiveness.

How can wisdom help you in your process of forgiving others?

FREEDOM

The Lord is the Spirit,
and where the Spirit of the Lord is,
there is freedom.

2 CORINTHIANS 3:17 NIV

My brothers and sisters, you were chosen to be free.
But don't use your freedom as an excuse to live under
the power of sin. Instead, serve one another in love.

GALATIANS 5:13 NIRV

"If the Son sets you free, you are truly free."

JOHN 8:36 NLT

We have freedom now,
because Christ made us free.
So stand strong.
Do not change and go back
into the slavery of the law.

GALATIANS 5:1 NCV

What a crazy, glorious thing it is to dwell on the expansive freedom you have bought for me by your blood, Jesus. Examine me now; whatever hinders me from walking in this freedom, whether it be legalism, addiction, craving approval, or anything else, reveal it to me. I pray that every chain will be broken completely. I want to live in the satisfying freedom of grace right now. You are full of life-giving joy, and you want to pour it out on me. May I use every freedom I already know for your glory.

How does choosing wisely show you are operating in freedom?

FRIENDSHIP

A friend loves you all the time,
and a brother helps in time of trouble.

PROVERBS 17:17 NCV

There are "friends" who destroy each other,
but a real friend sticks closer than a brother.

PROVERBS 18:24 NLT

"Greater love has no one than this:
to lay down one's life for one's friends.
You are my friends if you do what I command.
Instead, I have called you friends,
for everything that I learned from my Father
I have made known to you."

JOHN 15:13-15 NIV

"In everything, do to others
what you would want them to do to you."

MATTHEW 7:12 NIRV

You have called me friend, Jesus. What a profound, humbling statement. Thank you that you consider me your friend. Thank you that you have created me to live in community and relationship with others. Thank you for your body, the church, that you also designed and appointed for lifting each other up. In my relationships, give me the courage to be vulnerable, the wisdom to have boundaries, and the humility to serve in friendship. Make me iron that sharpens those around me and show me opportunities to be a friend to the lonely. If I'm struggling with lack of friendship right now, give me the courage to be the friend I need for someone else.

How do you rely on God's wisdom to help choose your friends?

GENEROSITY

Give generously to them and do so without a grudging
heart; then because of this the LORD your God will bless you
in all your work and in everything you put your hand to.

DEUTERONOMY 15:10 NIV

Each of you should give what you have
decided in your heart to give.
You shouldn't give if you don't want to.
You shouldn't give because you are forced to.
God loves a cheerful giver.

2 CORINTHIANS 9:7 NIRV

If you help the poor,
you are lending to the LORD—
and he will repay you!

PROVERBS 19:17 NLT

I praise you, oh generous God. You, having all things to give, gave what was most precious in your Son, Jesus. No greater generosity could be displayed than the love of one laying down his life. I confess, Lord, to holding back. Though all things are a gift from you, I often hold too tightly to the gifts, time, and resources you have lavished on me. Teach me the art of loosening my grasp. All things come from you, so grant me the wisdom to use what you have given me for your glory without hesitation.

How does using wisdom help you share with others?

GENTLENESS

"Accept my teachings and learn from me,
because I am gentle and humble in spirit,
and you will find rest for your lives."

MATTHEW 11:29 NCV

"Blessed are those who are humble.
They will be given the earth."

MATTHEW 5:5 NIRV

A gentle answer turns away wrath,
but a harsh word stirs up anger.

PROVERBS 15:1 NIV

Some people have gone astray without knowing it.
He is able to deal gently with them.
He can do that because he himself is weak.

HEBREWS 5:2 NIRV

Father, you are not a harsh God. You are not a dictator. You do not treat us with contempt. You are not quick to anger and you don't fly off the handle at me. I have so many wrong views of you embedded in my thoughts, Lord. I repent of these; remind me of your true character. You are abounding in love, patient, and great in mercy, with eyes that look on me with kindness and a voice that reassures like the rhythm of water.

Help me not to strive to be a nice person but renew my heart to treat others with true kindness and gentleness. Give me eyes to see them how you see them.

How does wisdom help you to be gentle with others?

GOODNESS

Everything God created is good,
and nothing is to be rejected
if it is received with thanksgiving.

1 TIMOTHY 4:4 NIV

Taste and see that the LORD is good.
Oh, the joys of those who take refuge in him!

PSALM 34:8 NLT

My brothers and sisters,
I am sure that you are full of goodness.
I know that you have all the knowledge you need
and that you are able to teach each other.

ROMANS 15:14 NCV

God, how can I know you are good in a world full of suffering that seems to scream otherwise? Are you good just because something pleasant happens or something awful is avoided? No, holy God, goodness is who you are. You are good in the deepest, muddiest pit, and you are good on the highest, soaring mountain. Your constant presence makes me aware of this. You never change, let go, quit, or bail out. I celebrate this about you. My heart fills with joy. Help me to see your goodness all around, in all that you created, and to rejoice at the reminders of your character in the world around me.

How does wisdom lead you to see the goodness of God in your life?

GRACE

From his fullness we have all received,
grace upon grace.

JOHN 1:16 NRSV

God gives us even more grace,
as the Scripture says,
"God is against the proud,
but he gives grace to the humble."

JAMES 4:6 NCV

Sin is no longer your master,
for you no longer live under the
requirements of the law.
Instead, you live under the freedom of God's grace.

ROMANS 6:14 NLT

Father, you show grace upon grace: layers and layers of it. It never expires and never runs out. I am so thankful for your bountiful grace! I daily face situations that cause me to become overwhelmed at my capacity to handle them. I need undeserved merit from you to go up against difficult situations. Keep my heart moving in the rhythm of your grace which always leads to softness of heart not a hard heart. Thank you for the tall, cool, refreshing cup of grace you serve me moment by moment. I will sing of your favor all day long and proclaim to those around me: my God is the God of grace!

**How can you apply grace more readily
if you are operating with wisdom?**

GRIEF

Those who sow in tears shall reap with shouts of joy.

PSALM 126:5 ESV

Let your steadfast love become my comfort
according to your promise to your servant.

PSALM 119:76 NRSV

"Come to me, all you who are weary and burdened,
and I will give you rest. Take my yoke upon you
and learn from me, for I am gentle and humble in heart,
and you will find rest for your souls."

MATTHEW 11:28-29 NIV

Every valley shall be raised up,
every mountain and hill made low;
the rough ground shall become level,
the rugged places a plain.

ISAIAH 40:4 NIV

You created me, Lord, a complex being with varied emotions. Thank you that in your wisdom you gave me tears and sadness to physically express the pain that is present in this world. Thank you that grief and lamentation are not foreign languages to you. You bore my grief, you carried my sorrow. I tear open my heart before you now; I rend it open and express every thought about this grief to you. Though I mourn, you are still good and you are still on your throne. You provide for me a table of abundance in the very presence of my enemies. May I not become so focused on the grievances around me that I forget at whose table I sit and who prepared the feast for me.

Does God's wisdom help you understand his comfort in times of pain?

GUIDANCE

Guide me in your truth and teach me,
for you are God my Savior,
and my hope is in you all day long.

PSALM 25:5 NIV

Wise people can also listen and learn;
even they can find good advice in these words.

PROVERBS 1:5 NCV

We can make our plans,
but the LORD determines our steps.

PROVERBS 16:9 NLT

Those who are led by the Spirit of God
are children of God.

ROMANS 8:14 NIRV

How wonderful a thought, Lord, that when I ask for direction from you, you freely give it. You are not unaware of even the smallest of needs that I may have. I pray that you go before me today, preparing a path. Though I sometimes try to rush ahead, keep me in rhythm with your steps, knowing that one day at a time is enough. Thank you for your body of believers: that you use us to help one another. Surround me with sound counsel and give me discernment between foolishness and godly wisdom.

What can God help guide you in today?

GUILT

God is faithful and fair. If we confess our sins,
he will forgive our sins. He will forgive every wrong
thing we have done. He will make us pure.

1 JOHN 1:9 NIRV

The LORD and King helps me.
He won't let me be dishonored.
So I've made up my mind to keep on serving him.
I know he won't let me be put to shame.

ISAIAH 50:7 NIRV

Those who go to him for help are happy,
and they are never disgraced.

PSALM 34:5 NCV

I have not achieved it,
but I focus on this one thing:
Forgetting the past and looking forward
to what lies ahead.

PHILIPPIANS 3:13 NLT

Wise are your promises and your Word, Lord. As far as the east is from the west, is how far you remove my sin from me. There is now no condemnation for me, as I am in you. You are faithful to forgive when I confess. All of these things are written in your Word and your Word is true. I praise you that your mercies are new every single morning. You make me as clean as fresh snow. Protect me now, from the arrows of shame and condemnation that threaten to stab my heart and wound me. Let your promises and truth be the only sounds I hear.

How does wisdom keep you from feeling guilt and shame?

HEALTH

The world and its desires pass away,
but whoever does the will of God lives forever.

1 John 2:17 NIV

Don't be wise in your own eyes.
Have respect for the LORD and avoid evil.
That will bring health to your body.
It will make your bones strong.

Proverbs 3:7-8 NIRV

I will never forget your commandments,
for by them you give me life.

Psalm 119:93 NLT

A happy heart is like good medicine,
but a broken spirit drains your strength.

Proverbs 17:22 NCV

Jehovah Rophe, you are our healer, You have been moving since the time of Adam to restore all things back to yourself. I praise you for sending your Son with healing on the fringes of his garment. All one woman had to do was reach out and she was healed. Today, Lord, I reach out my hands to you and pray for healing of my mind, body, and spirit. You alone have the power to heal, and I know it is your Spirit living within me. If it is your will, let healing flow like a river that I may glorify your name more.

What healing are you believing God for right now?

HONESTY

Keep me from deceitful ways;
be gracious to me and teach me your law.
I have chosen the way of faithfulness;
I have set my heart on your laws.

PSALM 119:29-30 NIV

"Everything that is hidden will become clear,
and every secret thing will be made known."

LUKE 8:17 NCV

The king is pleased with words from righteous lips;
he loves those who speak honestly.

PROVERBS 16:13 NLT

Instead, we will speak the truth in love.
So we will grow up in every way
to become the body of Christ.
Christ is the head of the body.

EPHESIANS 4:15 NIRV

You, Jesus, called yourself the truth. You, Holy Spirit, are the Spirit of truth. You, Father God, are an honest and true judge. Honesty is who you are. As for me, there is no part of me that is hidden from you. Search my heart and see if there is any deceit in me. Give me the courage to bring to the light anything I've been trying to hide. I want to live in the light, free from darkness. In my relationships, let there be complete illumination. Strengthen me when the temptation to speak or live in deceit arises.

Why is it wise to be honest?

HOPE

The LORD is good to those whose hope is in him,
to the one who seeks him.

LAMENTATIONS 3:25 NIV

Hope will never bring us shame.
That's because God's love
has poured into our hearts.
This happened through the Holy Spirit,
who has been given to us.

ROMANS 5:5 NIRV

The LORD's delight is in those who fear him,
those who put their hope in his unfailing love.

PSALM 147:11 NLT

God, I confess that hope can often feel like walking onto a rope bridge: shaky and unstable. I'm not even sure I want to step out. The reality is that hope in you is solid and firm, a stone I can build my whole life upon. Thank you that you are trustworthy, and if my hope is in you I can be confident in the future. I trust what I know about your character, what has been written in your Word about you. You are unshakeable, everlasting, honest, and true. Let hope arise within me again today when I find myself swayed by untrustworthy emotions or people's opinions.

How do you demonstrate wisdom when you place your hope in God?

HUMILITY

"Didn't I make everything by my power? That is how all things were created," announces the LORD. "The people I value are not proud. They are sorry for the wrong things they have done. They have great respect for what I say."

ISAIAH 66:2 NIRV

Humble yourselves before the Lord,
and he will lift you up.

JAMES 4:10 NIV

Pride will ruin people,
but those who are humble will be honored.

PROVERBS 29:23 NCV

The LORD has told you what is good,
and this is what he requires of you:
to do what is right, to love mercy,
and to walk humbly with your God.

MICAH 6:8 NLT

Jesus, you set the ultimate example. You stepped down from your throne of glory to walk among your creation, even to the extent of crucifixion. Help this be my attitude toward others. May I be ready and willing to give up my life, my comfort, my opinion, for others and serve in humility. As a member of your body, I can't think of myself alone. Give me wisdom that leans toward unity of your body. Give me eyes to see the people in my life as you see me: made in your image. When my outlook changes, give me a heart to serve.

How does wisdom help you practice humility?

IDENTITY

Do everything without grumbling or arguing,
so that you may become blameless and pure,
"children of God without fault
in a warped and crooked generation."
Then you will shine among them
like stars in the sky as you hold firmly
to the word of life.

PHILIPPIANS 2:14-16 NIV

I have been crucified with Christ;
and it is no longer I who live,
but Christ lives in me;
and the life which I now live in the flesh
I live by faith in the Son of God,
who loved me and gave Himself up for me.

GALATIANS 2:20 NASB

Your work on the cross and your defeat of sin and death changes who I am forever. As your child, teach me to hear your voice. Tune my ear to what you say about me. Let the truth of your Word be the only music I hear. Unchain me from any lies of the past regarding my identity; I repent of them and turn my eyes to yours for reassurance of truth. You are a good Father who created me uniquely, loves me deeply, and calls me your child. My identity and worth rests in you alone.

How does wisdom help you see yourself as God sees you?

INSPIRATION

The precepts of the LORD are right,
giving joy to the heart.
The commands of the LORD are radiant,
giving light to the eyes.

PSALM 19:8 NIV

Your laws are my treasure;
they are my heart's delight.

PSALM 119:111 NLT

The whole Bible was given to us by inspiration from God
and is useful to teach us what is true and to make us
realize what is wrong in our lives; it straightens us out
and helps us do what is right.

2 TIMOTHY 3:16 TLB

The default state of my heart is cold, God. Like building a fire on a chilly winter morning, let your words be the logs that fuel the start of my days. Search my heart, oh Lord; I confess my sin before you. Help me to remove the things that keep my heart's hearth cold. Holy Spirit, come and be the oxygen that provokes the sparks into flame. Let a fire roar within me now, warming up my heart and making me alive again to a new day in you. May your words and your spirit burn bright within me.

How do you find inspiration?

INTEGRITY

I know, my God, that you test the heart and are pleased
with integrity. All these things I have given willingly
and with honest intent.

1 CHRONICLES 29:17 NIV

"If you ignore the least commandment
and teach others to do the same,
you will be called the least in the Kingdom of Heaven.
But anyone who obeys God's laws and teaches them
will be called great in the Kingdom of Heaven."

MATTHEW 5:19 NLT

The honest person will live in safety,
but the dishonest will be caught.

PROVERBS 10:9 NCV

*Many are the voices and persuasions that try and convince
me of who I need to be these days, Lord. I confess how easy
it can be to try and portray myself a certain way or listen to
popular opinion about who you are and what your will is. I
want to be indifferent to popular opinion and in tune with
your Word. I want to be the same person, a person after your
heart, no matter the situation or circumstance. Help me to
be fully cohesive with your laws and statutes—to be found
genuine in a world full of fake.*

How do you show integrity when you choose to walk in the wisdom of God?

JOY

May the God of hope fill you with all joy and peace as you
trust in him, so that you may overflow with hope
by the power of the Holy Spirit.

ROMANS 15:13 NIV

"Don't be sad, because the joy of the LORD
will make you strong."

NEHEMIAH 8:10 NCV

The LORD is my strength and shield.
I trust him with all my heart.
He helps me, and my heart is filled with joy.
I burst out in songs of thanksgiving.

PSALM 28:7 NLT

Always be joyful because you belong to the Lord.
I will say it again. Be joyful!

PHILIPPIANS 4:4 NIRV

Forgive me, God, for my misconceptions about you. You are not a heavy taskmaster, but a joy-filled Father who rejoices over each lost person that comes to you. You delight in me. Singing and dancing and celebration occur in your presence at your glory! Display to my heart this glorious truth. What amazes me, Lord, is how your promises are eternal and solid while the world offers such temporary and flimsy relief. May my pursuit not be for fleeting happiness but a turning toward you for fullness of joy. Since joy is an eternal virtue, turn my vision to eternity. Enlighten me to anything that is hindering joy: bitterness, people-pleasing, performance-based living, ingratitude or anything else. Thank you for renewing my heart again.

What is one truly joyful moment you've had recently?

JUSTICE

He is the Rock. His works are perfect.

All his ways are right.

He is faithful.

He doesn't do anything wrong.

He is honest and fair.

DEUTERONOMY 32:4 NIRV

The LORD secures justice for the poor
and upholds the cause of the needy.

PSALM 140:12 NIV

There is joy for those
who deal justly with others
and always do what is right.

PSALM 106:3 NLT

Father, these truths about who you are provide a solid rock for the shaky ground I stand on. Because of who you are, my stance is confident reassurance of who I am. My eyes may find rest because I know you have my back. When I lose grace with those around me, judge my heart and find it true before you. You are not unfamiliar with betrayal, injustice, or slander. Lead me away from the temptation to play God; may you be the righteous judge in every situation. I lean upon your wisdom to bring justice.

Why is it wise to let God be the judge?

KINDNESS

Be kind to each other, tenderhearted,
forgiving one another,
just as God through Christ has forgiven you.

EPHESIANS 4:32 NLT

Kind people do themselves a favor,
but cruel people bring trouble on themselves.

PROVERBS 11:17 NCV

Do you disrespect God's great kindness and favor?
Do you disrespect God when he is patient with you?
Don't you realize that God's kindness is meant
to turn you away from your sins?

ROMANS 2:4 NIRV

Great is his love toward us,
and the faithfulness of the LORD endures forever.
Praise the LORD.

PSALM 117:2 NIV

God, you are not a harsh god. You are persevering in your patience toward me; overflowing mercy is on repeat. Open my eyes with the wisdom to see the destruction of sin and the kindness of your hand keeping me from continuing in it. As you lavish mercy upon me, may I be kind to those in my sphere. Let me not settle for polite or nice but seek after an atmosphere of kindness: true kindness points out sin and guides us to you. This brings you glory as repentance and mercy become like breathing.

How can you extend kindness as you are led by wisdom?

LONELINESS

"Teach them to obey everything that I have taught you,
and I will be with you always,
even until the end of this age."

MATTHEW 28:20 NCV

The LORD is near to all who call on him,
yes, to all who call on him in truth.

PSALM 145:18 NLT

Even if my father and mother abandon me,
the LORD will hold me close.

PSALM 27:10 NLT

"Be strong and courageous. Do not be afraid or terrified
because of them, for the LORD your God goes with you;
he will never leave you nor forsake you."

DEUTERONOMY 31:6 NIV

God who is near, who desires to abide and dwell with me, I confess and acknowledge my loneliness to you. You created me with a desire for intimacy and to be known. Help me discern between areas where this longing can be filled only by you (perhaps I am trying to fill it with earthly relationships and pleasures) and areas that you have desired it to be filled in community. Break down walls of fear and grant me the freedom of vulnerability: to live in relationship with your body and in communion with your Spirit.

How do you make wise choices when you are feeling lonely?

LOVE

Three things will last forever—
faith, hope, and love—
and the greatest of these is love.

1 CORINTHIANS 13:13 NLT

LORD, you are good. You are forgiving.
You are full of love for all who call out to you.

PSALM 86:5 NIRV

Fill us with your love every morning.
Then we will sing and rejoice all our lives.

PSALM 90:14 NCV

Let love and faithfulness never leave you;
bind them around your neck,
write them on the tablet of your heart.

PROVERBS 3:3 NIV

Abba, Father, you are perfect love. The greatest love was shown to mankind when you gave your only Son as the sacrifice for my sin. I confess my inability to love without you. Fill me with your Spirit that I may act in love toward those around me. Empower me with the discernment needed to know what it means to love according to 1 Corinthians 13. Let me not act selfishly but love you well by loving others well. Thank you that you are the only God who is abounding in love, that calls me his child, and desires relationship with me.

How does the love of God in your life help you to love others?

PATIENCE

Warn those who are lazy.
Encourage those who are timid.
Take tender care of those who are weak.
Be patient with everyone.

1 THESSALONIANS 5:14 NLT

Be like those who through faith and patience
will receive what God has promised.

HEBREWS 6:12 NCV

Be completely humble and gentle;
be patient, bearing with one another in love.

EPHESIANS 4:2 NIV

Anyone who is patient has great understanding.
But anyone who gets angry quickly
shows how foolish they are.

PROVERBS 14:29 NIRV

Father, in 1 Corinthians 13, you first paint the picture of unconditional love with the brushstroke of the word patience. It baffles me how patient you have been with me. Despite my sin, you love me no matter what. How kind you are toward me. Use every moment of my displayed impatience as a way to expose my selfishness: reshape me in holiness. The knowledge of your abounding mercy toward me spurs me on in offering this same grace to others.

How does wisdom increase your patience with others?

PEACE

"I have told you these things, so that you can have peace
because of me. In this world you will have trouble.
But be encouraged! I have won the battle over the world."

JOHN 16:33 NIRV

The LORD gives his people strength.
The LORD blesses them with peace.

PSALM 29:11 NLT

May the Lord of peace himself give you peace at all times
and in every way. The Lord be with all of you.

2 THESSALONIANS 3:16 NIV

"I am leaving you with a gift—peace of mind and heart.
And the peace I give is a gift the world cannot give.
So don't be troubled or afraid."

JOHN 14:27 NLT

Jehovah Shalom, you are peace and wholeness. True peace is found in right relationship with you. You have bridged the gap between God and man and now I can have peace in you. Thank you for providing a way! You enable me to live in peace in the most difficult of situations. This peace is found in your presence. In the decisions I face, give me the reassurance of peace. In trials, give me stillness of heart. Remove fear and plant your order in my mind. Humble me to live not at war with those around me but displaying your love.

**What kind of peace do you experience
when you respond to situations
with God's wisdom?**

PERSEVERANCE

In a race all the runners run. But only one gets the prize.
You know that, don't you? So run in a way
that will get you the prize.

1 CORINTHIANS 9:24-25 NIRV

I have tried hard to find you—
don't let me wander from your commands.

PSALM 119:10 NLT

I have fought the good fight,
I have finished the race,
I have kept the faith.

2 TIMOTHY 4:7 NCV

Let us not become weary in doing good,
for at the proper time
we will reap a harvest
if we do not give up.

GALATIANS 6:9 NIV

Lord, the word perseverance *brings to mind two parables you told that are recounted in the book of Luke. The persistent widow and the bold friend: both examples you gave of people who kept asking for what they needed. What this communicates to me, Lord, is that there is wisdom in praying even if it is for the same thing over a long period of time. May I be found faithful in the end: one who did not give up or shy away from coming to you and listened carefully for your response. Thank you for developing this character in me.*

What do you feel God is calling you to persevere in right now?

PRAYER

LORD, in the morning you hear my voice.
In the morning I pray to you.
I wait for you in hope.

PSALM 5:3 NIRV

Never stop praying.

1 THESSALONIANS 5:17 NIRV

The LORD does not listen to the wicked,
but he hears the prayers of those who do right.

PROVERBS 15:29 NCV

Come, let us bow down in worship,
let us kneel before the LORD our Maker.

PSALM 95:6 NIV

Father, I am overwhelmed with gratitude that you are the living God who hears me. I come before your throne now with boldness, with confidence because you are alive. You awoke from death and defeated it. Though I come boldly, I also come in humility, as children approach their father. You see me, Abba, with eyes of mercy. You give good gifts not stones. You are trustworthy and true and big enough to handle all my doubts, fears, and anxieties. You request that I tell you about them. Will you align my thoughts of you with truth? Will you teach me to pray in light of what your character is truly like? I submit my words and my thoughts to your will.

What is wisdom prompting you to pray for right now?

PROTECTION

My God is my rock. I can run to him for safety.

He is my shield and my saving strength,

my defender and my place of safety.

The LORD saves me from those who want to harm me.

2 SAMUEL 22:3 NCV

The LORD is good, a refuge in times of trouble.

He cares for those who trust in him.

NAHUM 1:7 NIV

We are pushed hard from all sides.

But we are not beaten down.

We are bewildered. But that doesn't make us lose hope.

Others make us suffer. But God does not desert us.

We are knocked down. But we are not knocked out.

2 CORINTHIANS 4:8-9 NIRV

Lord, so often I am guilty of trying to rise up in my own wisdom and strength to take care of myself and my problems. I repent of my independent streak. Strength lies in reliance on you, and I fight my battles through prayer, worship, and submission to you. Help me to see that you are the true victor, and the enemy is spiritual. Protect me from the attacks of the enemy that make me pridefully think I can do this life alone. These trials make me want to lash out at those around me, to start fighting in the physical. Help me not to lose hope in your goodness.

**How hard is it for you to lay down
your battle plan and let God
be your wise protector?**

PROVISION

All scripture is inspired by God and is useful for
teaching, for reproof, for correction, and for training in
righteousness, so that everyone who belongs to God may
be proficient, equipped for every good work.

2 TIMOTHY 3:16–17 NRSV

May he give you the power to accomplish all the
good things your faith prompts you to do.

2 THESSALONIANS 1:11 NLT

We are God's handiwork,
created in Christ Jesus to do good works,
which God prepared in advance for us to do.

EPHESIANS 2:10 NIV

The LORD reached out his hand and touched my mouth
and said to me, "I have put my words in your mouth."

JEREMIAH 1:9 NIV

Jehovah Jireh, the God who provides, you are the God of majestic splendor and abundance. There is no mountain too high, no road to crooked, no task too small, and no necessity unseen by you in life. I repent, Lord, of striving to do everything alone my way. You are a miracle worker, and you go before me on the path of life: a true good shepherd and guide. I repent for thinking that you are holding out on me. Will you move this mountain today? Thank you for your generosity and care for me.

How have you seen God provide for you lately?

PURPOSE

You have been raised up with Christ.
So think about things that are in heaven.
That is where Christ is.
He is sitting at God's right hand.

Colossians 3:1 nirv

We know that in all things God works
for the good of those who love him,
who have been called according to his purpose.

Romans 8:28 niv

My child, pay attention to my words;
listen closely to what I say.
Don't ever forget my words; keep them always in mind.

Proverbs 4:20-21 ncv

God, your plans cannot be faltered. You are full of wisdom and you are working in my world. Thank you, Jesus, that by your blood I am a child of God whose citizenship is in heaven. By making me a new creation, equipping me with unique gifts, you have placed me in this particular time and place to work for you. Help me to see where you want me to be light. Give me discernment to know how to be salt. I am willing, Lord, use me as a vessel for your glory.

How does wisdom help you discover the purpose God has for your life?

RELAXATION

Blessed is the one who trusts in the LORD,
whose confidence is in him.
They will be like a tree planted by the water
that sends out its roots by the stream.
It does not fear when heat comes;
its leaves are always green.
It has no worries in a year of drought
and never fails to bear fruit.

JEREMIAH 17:7–8 NIV

"Let not your heart be troubled;
you believe in God, believe also in Me.
In My Father's house are many mansions.
I go to prepare a place for you.
And if I go and prepare a place for you,
I will come again and receive you to Myself;
that where I am, there you may be also."

JOHN 14:1–3 NKJV

Father of Sabbath, you have ordained for me times of rest. I hear the frantic cry of culture to hustle, contrasting with the gentle eyes of my Savior beckoning me to relax. Grant me the wisdom to carve out time to rest as you did when you created the world. Bring to a halt the endless running of my thoughts; help me to practice the art of being still. May this rest remind me of what is to come: the eternal release of all burdens and cares and the anticipation of being in your presence forevermore. Let this rest strengthen my soul and refocus my eyes for the work ahead.

How can you practice relaxing in God's presence?

RELATIONSHIPS

Two are better than one,
because they have a good return for their labor:
If either of them falls down,
one can help the other up.

ECCLESIASTES 4:9–10 NIV

Perfume and incense bring joy to the heart,
and the pleasantness of a friend
springs from their heartfelt advice.

PROVERBS 27:9 NIV

Love each other with genuine affection,
and take delight in honoring each other.

ROMANS 12:10 NLT

Jesus, friend of sinners, I am humbled by your choice to enter into relationship with me. I am in awe of the perfection of unity in the holy trinity, the love that exists between Father, Son, and Spirit. I confess my desires to insulate my heart from interaction with others or even with you. Help me open the doors of my heart to those around me. Give me the grace to show interest in others, to have mercy on their shortcomings, and the courage to share my own. Thank you that in your wisdom you created us to be in community and not alone.

How does wisdom help you in your relationships with others?

RELIABILITY

"All people are like grass.
All their glory is like the flowers
in the field. The grass dries up.
The flowers fall to the ground.
But the word of the LORD lasts forever."

1 PETER 1:24-25 NIRV

He will give eternal life to those who keep on doing good,
seeking after the glory and honor and immortality
that God offers.

ROMANS 2:7 NLT

You are near, LORD,
and all your commands are true.
Long ago I learned from your statutes
that you established them to last forever.

PSALM 119:151-152 NIV

Faithful and true God, you are the rock of ages. There is none as solid and trustworthy as you. You always have been, and always will be. Your promises toward me remain, and you are faithful to fulfill them. I repent of my independent spirit—the part of me that wants to rely on no one and trust nothing— that ugly pride that rears up. Thank you for your patience toward me and your faithfulness to me. Help me to trust; break down the walls of independence and self-reliance that hinder me from leaning completely on your everlasting arms.

How does it make you feel knowing you can rely on God for everything?

RELIEF

"Come to me, all you who are weary and burdened,
and I will give you rest. Take my yoke upon you and learn
from me, for I am gentle and humble in heart,
and you will find rest for your souls."

MATTHEW 11:28–29 NIV

"I am the Alpha and the Omega—
the Beginning and the End.
To all who are thirsty I will give freely
from the springs of the water of life."

REVELATION 21:6 NLT

I prayed to the LORD, and he answered me.
He freed me from all my fears.
Those who look to him for help will be radiant with joy.

PSALM 34:4–5 NLT

Father of light, creator of the brilliant sun and the reflective moon, I am overwhelmed by the darkness that surrounds me. It is difficult to remember what the warmth of light feels like, what the sound of laughter is. My eyes are blinded to your movement. Remove the veil from my eyes; let your will be illuminated before me. Restore to me the beautiful sound of laughter and joy. Wrap your light around me like a blanket of warmth and stir up the fire in my soul again. You will bring this time of suffering to an end and restore all things. Let that hope be a beacon of relief in my despair today.

How can the wisdom of God offer relief in your current situation?

RESPECT

Show respect for all people:
Love the brothers and sisters of God's family,
respect God, honor the king.

1 PETER 2:17 NCV

Don't do anything only to get ahead.
Don't do it because you are proud.
Instead, be humble.
Value others more than yourselves.

PHILIPPIANS 2:3 NIRV

Acknowledge those who work hard among you,
who care for you in the Lord and who admonish you.
Hold them in the highest regard in love because of
their work. Live in peace with each other.

1 THESSALONIANS 5:12-13 NIV

God, you are sovereign over all the world—a God of order and not chaos. You have ordained leadership and authority. I confess my natural inclination is rebellion. I am prone toward independence from you and from my fellow man. I repent of this and ask you to humble me. Give me respectful words to say to those in authority around me. Empower me to look to you for justice when I feel wronged. When I don't agree with those in authority, guide me in truth and wisdom for how to handle it. Thank you for the order you have placed in this world.

Why is it wise to show respect to the authority figures in your life?

RESTORATION

He has saved us and called us to a holy life—
not because of anything we have done
but because of his own purpose and grace.

2 TIMOTHY 1:9 NIV

Since we have been made right in God's sight by faith,
we have peace with God because of what Jesus Christ our
Lord has done for us. Because of our faith, Christ has
brought us into this place of undeserved privilege where
we now stand, and we confidently and joyfully look
forward to sharing God's glory.

ROMANS 5:1—2 NLT

"Let us praise the Lord, the God of Israel,
because he has come to help his people
and has given them freedom.
He has given us a powerful Savior."

LUKE 1:68-69 NCV

Father, when a category five storm arrives, its destruction is evident. Broken buildings, trees torn from their roots, chaos, and unrest rule the air. This is my world when my sin and others' sins blow through. It's a mess, Lord, and I feel the helpless ache in the middle of it all. But this is not the end of the story. You are the God who restores my soul. You make all things new, and you will set this world completely right and aligned with your glory in due time. Thank you that you do not abandon me to the storm but rebuild my broken world with grandeur. Will you move with your restoring power in my life today?

How does God's wisdom help you experience restoration in your life?

REWARD

Work willingly at whatever you do, as though you were
working for the Lord rather than for people. Remember
that the Lord will give you an inheritance as your reward,
and that the Master you are serving is Christ.

COLOSSIANS 3:23-24 NLT

"Love your enemies, do good to them,
and lend to them without expecting to get anything back.
Then your reward will be great,
and you will be children of the Most High,
because he is kind to the ungrateful and wicked."

LUKE 6:35 NIV

Without faith it is impossible to please God.
Those who come to God must believe that he exists.
And they must believe that he rewards those
who look to him.

HEBREWS 11:6 NIRV

King of kings, your splendor is on display in the world around us; everything was created by you and for you and belongs to you. You greatly reward those who seek you. I confess I often settle for earthly rewards that don't remain. Let not my heart be satisfied with power, praise, or pleasure. Earthly treasures are temporary; your rewards are eternal. Thank you for the hope of the promise of what is to come. I am a sojourner in this land, and I am not home until I am with you. Along this road, let me hold onto nothing and look forward to everything.

How does wisdom help you remain diligent in seeking your heavenly reward?

SAFETY

The LORD also will be a refuge for the oppressed,
A refuge in times of trouble.
Those who know Your name will put their trust in You;
For You, LORD, have not forsaken those who seek You.

PSALM 9:9–10 NKJV

The name of the LORD is a strong tower;
The righteous runs into it and is safe.

PROVERBS 18:10 NASB

Wherever I am, though far away at the ends of the earth,
I will cry to you for help.
When my heart is faint and overwhelmed,
lead me to the mighty, towering Rock of safety.
For you are my refuge, a high tower
where my enemies can never reach me.

PSALM 61:2-3 TLB

Creation groans for its redemption still, Lord. Reminders of sin lie all about me in the tragedies, crime, injustice, and upheaval I see and feel. We are frail, yet you are solid. I can be surrounded by enemies, yet you and your mercies are abundantly available. When I feel unsafe, fill me with your peace. When I don't know what to do, grant me good judgement. I know you hear my cries and respond; you are not deaf to them or turned away from them. Thank you for being a God who hears and is near. This is true safety.

How does God's wisdom help you feel safe?

SATISFACTION

Because your love is better than life,
my lips will glorify you.
I will praise you as long as I live,
and in your name I will lift up my hands.
I will be fully satisfied as with the richest of foods;
with singing lips my mouth will praise you.

<small>PSALM 63:3–5 NIV</small>

"Give, and it will be given to you.
A good measure, pressed down,
shaken together and running over,
will be poured into your lap.
For with the measure you use,
it will be measured to you."

<small>LUKE 6:38 NIV</small>

Whoever pursues righteousness and love
finds life, prosperity and honor.

<small>PROVERBS 21:21 NIV</small>

Oh God my redeemer, I am overwhelmed when I think about the radical change you have brought to my life. I was a slave, blind and broken, wallowing in the filth of sin. You redeemed me, washed me clean, clothed me in new robes, bound up my wounds, and healed my vision. I am free and all I need is you. You are my home. You are the land and the sky I was made to dwell in and beneath. Thank you for your favor toward me. May my soul find contentment in you alone every moment.

How can you be satisfied with all God has given you?

SERVING

Each of you should use whatever gift you have received
to serve others, as faithful stewards of God's grace in its
various forms. If anyone serves, they should do so with
the strength God provides, so that in all things God may
be praised through Jesus Christ.

1 PETER 4:10-11 NIV

Always give yourselves fully to the work of the Lord,
because you know that your labor in the Lord
is not in vain.

1 CORINTHIANS 15:58 NIV

You were called to freedom…
do not use your freedom
as an opportunity for the flesh,
but through love serve one another.

GALATIANS 5:13 ESV

You have bestowed upon me good gifts, Father. Thank you!
This wisdom, knowledge, and special gifting from you is not
the end game for my glory. Keep me from the temptation to use
these gifts to impress those around me or to gain advantage
over others. Show me where I may use my gifts to edify and
love others. Shield me from burnout, which comes when I
rise up to do things in my own power. Give me the fortitude to
serve and the knowledge of when to rest as well.

How can you be wise
about how you serve today?

STRENGTH

God is our refuge and strength,
an ever-present help in trouble.

PSALM 46:1-3 NIV

The Lord is faithful; he will strengthen you
and guard you from the evil one.

2 THESSALONIANS 3:3 NIRV

Don't be afraid, for I am with you.
Don't be discouraged, for I am your God.
I will strengthen you and help you.
I will hold you up with my victorious right hand.

ISAIAH 41:10 NLT

You are a strong tower, Lord, and when I abide in you, then I am strong. I recognize my own weakness apart from you—that I am merely flesh. But you are all-knowing and all-powerful. Apart from you I can do no good thing. Wisdom speaks to me that it is in this recognition of weakness that you make me strong. Help my spiritual muscles, Lord. Give them a workout! Have them grow as I find myself in situations that I can choose my own strength or yours. Give me the humility to rely on you.

How does wisdom make you feel strong?

STRESS

Praise the LORD, my soul;
all my inmost being, praise his holy name.
Praise the LORD, my soul,
and forget not all his benefits—
who forgives all your sins
and heals all your diseases,
who redeems your life from the pit
and crowns you with love and compassion,
who satisfies your desires with good things
so that your youth is renewed like the eagle's.

PSALM 103:1–5 NIV

Commit your actions to the LORD.
and your plans will succeed.

PROVERBS 16:3 NLT

Be still, my soul. I feel like a boiling pot sometimes, Jesus. Steam rising, everything swirling, about to run over, and ruin everything. I feel like a one-person circus act: plates spinning, crowd watching, waiting for me to fall. Help me to be still, Lord. To know that no matter what I face, worry and stress add nothing. Calm the boiling pot. Help me give the plates to you. Lock eyes with mine and remind me that you are in control of my life. Lift me up again, set my feet on a straight path, and be ever near as I face each task.

How can God's wisdom help you to reduce the stress in your life?

TEACHING

All scripture is inspired by God
and is useful for teaching,
for reproof, for correction,
and for training in righteousness,
so that everyone who belongs to God may be proficient,
equipped for every good work.

2 Timothy 3:16-17 NRSV

Let each generation tell its children of your mighty acts;
let them proclaim your power.

Psalm 145:4 NLT

"Go therefore and make disciples of all the nations,
baptizing them in the name of the Father and of the Son
and of the Holy Spirit, teaching them to observe
all things that I have commanded you."

Matthew 28:19-20 NKJV

What a privilege it is to read your Word, God. Thank you for giving me this book, your Holy Scripture, to equip me. Help me not to take for granted the access I have to read, study, and share your life-giving words with those around me. Surrounded by thirsty people, I have living water. Remind me to offer it! Hide your Word in my heart that I have it readily available to share. Thank you for your Spirit that guides me in truth. I don't want to take this task lightly, and I don't want to be overcome by fear. Your words are the words of life. Strengthen me to share them with all.

How can you pass wisdom along to others?

THANKFULNESS

I have not stopped giving thanks for you,
remembering you in my prayers.

EPHESIANS 1:16 NIV

Giving thanks is a sacrifice that truly honors me.
If you keep to my path,
I will reveal to you the salvation of God.

PSALM 50:23 NLT

Rejoice always, pray continually,
give thanks in all circumstances;
for this is God's will for you in Christ Jesus.

1 THESSALONIANS 5:16–18 NIV

Give thanks as you enter the gates of his temple.
Give praise as you enter its courtyards.
Give thanks to him and praise his name.

PSALM 100:4 NIRV

I look around and see so much I have to give thanks for, Lord. I look back and in remembrance praise you for each step of faithfulness you have had in my life. You have never left, you've always provided, and you stayed true to your promises. Gratitude grows wisdom. It shows me that everything I have is a gift from you—the very oxygen I breathe. If I want to grow in wisdom, I have to grow in thankfulness. Teach me to hold my tongue of complaints and overflow with thankfulness instead.

What can you thank God for right now?

TRUST

Those who know the LORD trust him,
because he will not leave those who come to him.

PSALM 9:10 NCV

I trust in you, LORD. I say, "You are my God."
My whole life is in your hands.
Save me from the hands of my enemies.
Save me from those who are chasing me.

PSALM 31:14-15 NIV

Yes, the LORD is for me; he will help me.
I will look in triumph at those who hate me.
It is better to take refuge in the LORD
than to trust in people.

PSALM 118:7-8 NLT

Christ, you are the cornerstone, a firm foundation. As the solid rock upon which the entire church is built, it is evident to me that you are trustworthy. Your Word is full of promises and prophecies about you as Messiah—all of which have been kept and will be fulfilled. The evidence is stacked in your favor! Wisdom tells me that you are a trustworthy God. With this in mind, I ask you to grow faith in me. There are areas that I don't yet trust you with. Show them to me, and grow my faith to be able to give them to you.

How does wisdom help you identify who is trustworthy?

TRUTH

"When he, the Spirit of truth, comes,
he will guide you into all the truth."

JOHN 16:13 NIV

The very essence of your words is truth;
all your just regulations will stand forever.

PSALM 119:160 NLT

"If you abide in My word,
you are My disciples indeed.
And you shall know the truth,
and the truth shall make you free."

JOHN 8:31-32 NKJV

Teach me your way, O LORD, that I may walk in your truth;
unite my heart to fear your name.

PSALM 86:11 ESV

God, what a contrast there is between you and the enemy. You are the truth; he is the father of lies. You have promised that your truth will set me free, that your Spirit will guide me in truth. In truth is wisdom and understanding. When things feel unclear, when I encounter fear or betrayal, I know that you are trustworthy. Bring truth to my mind; remind me of your words. Train me in knowing your voice and discerning between truth and lies. Lead me away from the temptation of using deception for a shortcut or for my own gain and give me the courage and clarity to speak truth in every situation.

What steps can you take to be more truthful in your everyday life?

UNDERSTANDING

Understanding is like a fountain of life
to those who have it.
But foolish people are punished
for the foolish things they do.

PROVERBS 16:22 NIRV

The teaching of your word gives light,
so even the simple can understand.

PSALM 119:130 NLT

Give me understanding,
so that I may keep your law
and obey it with all my heart.

PSALM 119:34 NIV

Don't act thoughtlessly,
but understand what the Lord wants you to do.

EPHESIANS 5:17 NLT

God, what a blessing it is to have your holy Word, written out in my native tongue and readily available to me. Through this I gain knowledge of your character, your ways, the history of your people, and your plan of redemption for mankind. Thank you for the gift of your Holy Spirit that brings to me understanding of these words. Holy Spirit, move in me to take this knowledge and understanding and apply it as wisdom. To act out obedience to your Word. In every situation I face, help me discern your movement, presence, and will.

How are wisdom and understanding different?

VICTORY

You can prepare a horse for the day of battle.
But the power to win comes from the LORD.

PROVERBS 21:31 NIRV

Every child of God defeats this evil world,
and we achieve this victory through our faith.

1 JOHN 5:4 NLT

From the LORD comes deliverance.
May your blessing be on your people.

PSALM 3:8 NIV

"The LORD your God is the one who goes with you
to fight for you against your enemies to give you victory."

DEUTERONOMY 20:4 NIV

Victory has been won by you, oh Lord! On your side, I am on the winning team. I can look evil in the eye and say, "It doesn't look good for you or your kind; I know who wins." No matter what battle I am fighting right now, for relationships, for a sin struggle, for health, or for provision, I choose not to focus on the clanking swords in front of me. Instead, lift my eyes to you, my King, to see that the battle is won. You hold the keys of sin and death and you are the hero of this tale.

How does wisdom help you experience victory in your life?

WHOLENESS

He will take our weak mortal bodies and change them
into glorious bodies like his own, using the same power
with which he will bring everything under his control.

PHILIPPIANS 3:21 NLT

Celebrate with praises the God and Father of our Lord
Jesus Christ, who has shown us his extravagant mercy.
For his fountain of mercy has given us a new life—
we are reborn to experience a living, energetic hope
through the resurrection of Jesus Christ from the dead.
We are reborn into a perfect inheritance that can never
perish, never be defiled, and never diminish. It is
promised and preserved forever in the heavenly realm
for you! Through our faith, the mighty power of God
constantly guards us until our full salvation is ready to be
revealed in the last time.

1 PETER 1:3—5 TPT

God, when a glass is dropped, I am unable to piece the shards together again. This picture may seem hopeless, yet you change the image. You have promised to take every sliver and make me whole again. You waste nothing in my life. When I try to repair the brokenness on my own, I end up cut and bleeding. By your wounds and your blood, however, I am healed and whole again. This life feels fragmented, but your promise stands that in heaven my body and mind will be completely whole in you. Thank you for that truth.

How does understanding eternal wholeness benefit you in this life?

WORRY

Turn your worries over to the LORD.
He will keep you going.
He will never let godly people be shaken.

PSALM 55:22 NIRV

"Who of you by worrying
can add a single hour to your life?"

LUKE 12:25 NIV

Worry weighs a person down;
an encouraging word cheers a person up.

PROVERBS 12:25 NLT

Do not worry about anything,
but pray and ask God for everything you need,
always giving thanks.
And God's peace, which is so great
we cannot understand it,
will keep your hearts and minds in Christ Jesus.

PHILIPPIANS 4:6-7 NCV

God, may my worries be like an alarm in my head. Let them become my prayer alarm clock. May they awaken the desire to pray, to come into your presence. I know I can do nothing and change no circumstance through worry, but you hear my prayers and work through them to move mountains. May I redeem these thoughts by handing them over to you. Thank you that you recycle my worries into peace that floods through me. You protect me from straying down anxious roads. I trust you to make a way, and I know that you are a good Father.

How can you apply wisdom to your worries today?

BroadStreet Publishing Group, LLC.
Savage, Minnesota, USA
Broadstreetpublishing.com

Prayers & Promises for Wisdom

© 2020 by BroadStreet Publishing®

978-1-4245-6063-9
978-1-4245-6064-6 (ebook)

Prayers composed by Rachel Flores.

Design by Chris Garborg | garborgdesign.com
Editorial services by Michelle Winger | literallyprecise.com

Printed in China.

20 21 22 23 24 25 26   7 6 5 4 3 2 1